Dr Lala Manners

fantastic ideas for
getting children active

FEATHERSTONE

FEATHERSTONE
Bloomsbury Publishing Plc
50 Bedford Square, London, WC1B 3DP, UK

BLOOMSBURY, FEATHERSTONE and the Feather logo are trademarks of Bloomsbury Publishing Plc

First published in Great Britain 2020 by Bloomsbury Publishing Plc

A catalogue record for this book is available from the British Library

ISBN: PB: 978-1-4729-7185-2; ePDF: 978-1-4729-7184-5

2 4 6 8 10 9 7 5 3 1

Series design: Lynda Murray

Printed and bound in China by Leo Paper Products, Heshan, Guangdong

To find out more about our authors and books visit www.bloomsbury.com and sign up for our newsletters

Contents

Introduction

Life for young children is all about being physical. The ability to successfully join in, keep up and contribute impacts on their social skills, language development and emotional wellbeing. Having a reliably strong, balanced, agile and coordinated body will determine what they play, who they play with, how they play, where they play and the resources they choose. When children are confident and competent physically it has a profoundly positive impact on their general health and wellbeing.

We often assume that children will just 'get on with it': that they will engage in physical play for as long as allowed, creating their own opportunities to be active, then mercifully flop into bed to sleep soundly. For a multitude of reasons, this is no longer the case. We as adults now need to play a much more meaningful and proactive role in ensuring children experience the quality and quantity of physical activity that effectively supports their overall development. You can use all the ideas in this book as a base to create your own portfolio of activities.

When to get active

The World Health Organisation and many countries have produced activity guidelines for the early years. The main message of these guidelines is move more, sit less and sleep well. 180 minutes of physical activity spread throughout the day is recommended by all models – the more, the better.

The activities included in this book may be enjoyed by all age groups at any time of day but there are suggestions for the age groups to which they may be best suited. There are some energetic ideas to get everyone moving in the morning, more challenging physical activities for the middle of the day and a range of ideas that highlight body-awareness and breathing to help wind down at the end of the day.

Some tips before you start

- Try to maximise the time and opportunities for all children from birth to five years to be as active as possible throughout the day. Provide a varied combination of free play, spontaneous, semi-structured and structured activities.

- Aim to use easily accessible and free-to-source materials that children can find in different environments, e.g. at home and school.

- Tune into children's physical needs and requests and go along with their ideas if appropriate.

- Notice any particular likes or dislikes the children express: be sensitive and supportive.

- Try not to move on too quickly from one idea to the next. Children need time to settle into an activity and to properly explore and experiment with materials – getting better at anything requires continual repetition and practice.

- It is important to include an element of risk, challenge and adventure if/when appropriate.

- Remember that any language acquired in a movement context is immediately relevant and meaningful.

- Progression in physical development is only sometimes linear: regressions and plateaus are equally important and progress can take many forms, for example new friendships or language. Children will get to where they need and want to be in good time, provided they experience plenty of opportunities to move and have your continual support and encouragement.

Key messages

Value children's physical skills: they are a huge source of untapped learning opportunities, particularly for supporting language, communication, social and emotional skills.

Trust that an element of risk and challenge is positive and that children can make the right personal decisions as they become physically more confident and competent, creative and adaptive.

Understand how, when and where skills are acquired and developed over time. Remember that age is probably the least relevant factor and that milestones are not millstones!

The structure of the book

Before you start any activity, read through everything on the page so you are familiar with the whole activity and what you might need to plan in advance. The pages are all organised in the same way.

What you need lists the resources required for the activity. You should also ensure the space you're using is always clean and hazard-free.

What to do provides step-by-step instructions.

Health & Safety: In many cases there are no specific hazards involved in completing the activity, and your usual health and safety measures should be enough. In others there are particular issues to be noted and addressed.

What's in it for the children? lists some of the benefits children will gain from the activities and how this will contribute to their learning.

Taking it forward gives ideas for additional activities on the same theme, or for developing the activity further. These will be particularly useful for things that have gone especially well or where children show a real interest. In many cases they use the same resources, and in every case they have been designed to extend learning and broaden the children's experiences.

Top tips give a brief word of advice or helpful tip that could make all the difference to the experience of the activity for you and your children.

Movement and melody for all ages

Tips for moving to music

What you need:

- Speakers

What to do:

1. Identify musical genres, songs and rhymes that the children are already familiar with. Source music from around the world and ask parents or carers if they have any favourites.

2. Identify the optimum times within your setting in which music may be used most effectively to energise, calm, sooth, or inspire.

3. **The first year:**

   a. Source familiar materials babies can make different sounds with, e.g. spoons and pots, and encourage movements like patting, knocking and rubbing.

   b. Move to music by rocking, swaying and swinging with them. Sing to them whenever possible – make up your own rhymes!

4. **1–3 years:**

   a. Children will begin to mirror your movements and enjoy joining in. Create short movement sequences they can practise easily, e.g. a combination of claps, jumps, twirls, stretches and stillness.

   b. Encourage children to make different sounds with familiar materials.

   c. Sing together and say rhymes that are easy for the children to repeat independently.

5. **3–5 years:**

   a. Children will begin to enjoy music as a framework for movement, for example, they can play music-based games like musical statues.

   b. Create rhythmic sequences with hands and feet that children can repeat and teach to others.

   c. Introduce percussion instruments as an accompaniment to music, particularly handmade ones.

What's in it for the children?

Children may explore 'cultural capital' through exposure to different musical genres. Physical skills are rehearsed and refined and new vocabulary may be introduced in a meaningful and relevant context.

Taking it forward

- Create more complex and longer movement sequences to music, for example with different speeds or materials e.g. ribbons and scarves.

- Children may eventually perform their own poems and stories with a musical element.

Touch time, on backs

Positive, enjoyable touch

What you need:

- A clean, safe surface (cot, floor or sofa)
- Minimal clothing

Top tip

Observe likes and dislikes, for example some children dislike being tickled or blown on.

What's in it for the children?

Positive, enjoyable touch is a critical factor in supporting early overall development. Children gain early experience of 'the complete learning package' – matching movement, language and feeling. They become aware of their 'body maps' – where body parts are in relation to each other – and the proprioceptive sense is stimulated, enabling them to establish where they are in space.

Taking it forward

- As children get stronger and more agile, encourage big body movements such as kicking, waving, or holding toes independently.

- Encourage children to use different hand movements on *your* body by asking 'Can you pat my arm/tickle my ear/rub my tummy?'

What to do:

1. Allow time for sustained eye contact and ensure the atmosphere is unhurried and calm.

2. Use a range of different hand movements, e.g. patting, stroking, brushing, tickling, rubbing, or walking fingers, as you move up and down the child's body. Don't forget very small body parts, e.g. ear lobes, heels, or elbows.

3. Describe what you are doing using a calm voice. For example, 'Now I'm going to pat your tummy/tickle your toes/rub your chest.'

4. Include rhymes that children can become familiar with and can anticipate the end, e.g. 'Round and round the garden, like a teddy bear.'

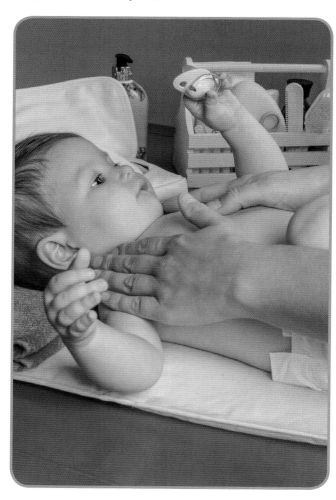

Tummy time

Enjoy short periods on tummies

What you need:

- A clean, clear surface
- Minimal clothing

What's in it for the children?

Being on their tummies is a very important position for children to experience: daily and frequently. It encourages the lifting of the head to 45 degrees and impacts on eye skills, balance and motivation to become independently mobile as they begin to push up on their hands. Tummy time also aligns hips to 90 degrees (needed for later fluent walking) and stabilises the shoulder girdle that impacts on later writing skills.

Taking it forward

- This is perfect preparation for future locomotor skills, e.g. crawling, cruising and walking.

Health & Safety

Don't leave children unsupervised. Check feet on baby grows are not getting too tight.

What to do:

1. Encourage babies from around seven weeks onwards to enjoy being on their tummies for short periods when they are fully awake. Aim for 30 minutes tummy time over the course of a day. Some experts believe it may be best introduced around six months when they can roll over independently.

2. Source a range of different materials and surfaces for babies to lie on, e.g. carpet, velvet, lycra or grass, and observe their reactions. Do they have any particular favourites?

3. If the baby dislikes the floor, or there isn't an appropriate surface, tummy time can also be experienced by placing the baby over one arm or by lying the baby on the adult's tummy, over a ball, or the arm of a chair.

Top tip

Don't leave babies in the same position for longer than 15 minutes – as they grow and develop they will naturally change position by themselves every two minutes.

Water play (small scale)

Washing individual body parts

What you need:

- Washing up bowl, filled with no more than five centimetres of warm water
- Small sponge or flannel

What to do:

1. Invite the child or children to sit near the washing up bowl.
2. Start with the hands. Dip the sponge or flannel in the water and carefully wash each finger, describing what you are doing, e.g. rubbing or dabbing.
3. Now examine different parts of the hand (wrist/ knuckles/nails/thumb/palm), clearly saying each part as you touch it.
4. Move on to the head. Describe different parts of the face as you wash them (cheeks/chin/nose/forehead/ ears/neck).
5. Encourage children to wiggle and stretch vigorously as you wash different parts.
6. Play peek-a-boo with the sponge or flannel (the most popular game ever!)
7. Remember to maintain eye contact and keep your voice calm and low.

What's in it for the children?

This activity encourages children's interest in their bodies: how do body parts connect and what can different parts do? Children hear new vocabulary in a relevant and meaningful context.

Taking it forward

- Ask children if they can identify their own body parts by pointing to them as you say them.
- Ask children if they can demonstrate different actions with the sponge or flannel, e.g. rubbing, squeezing or dabbing.
- If children are wearing minimal clothing, they could wash their whole bodies!

Sling time

What do you see?

What you need:

- **A comfortable baby sling or carrier**

Top tip ⭐

Aim to carry a child for no longer than 10 – 15 minutes when they are awake and alert.

What's in it for the children?

Carrying young children for short periods is very useful for those who may experience difficulty settling sometimes. Children also benefit from experiencing a different view of the environment. The spine is adequately supported and the surrounding muscles are working to maintain an upright position.

Taking it forward

- Play some appropriate music that you can both move (and maybe sing) to.

What to do:

1. Source a baby sling or carrier that is the right size and fit for you and the child.

2. Carry the child facing outwards. Ensure their legs and arms can move freely and their torso is lightly supported. Make sure you are both completely comfortable.

3. Move around the immediate environment and describe what you see, hear and smell. Ensure physical contact is maintained as you rub their feet and touch their hands and head occasionally.

4. Encourage the child to say hello to anyone you encounter: adults, children or animals. Describe who they are, what they are wearing and what role they play in your setting.

Swing time

Lift and swing children gently

What you need:

- Space to move freely

What to do:

1. Place the child along one of your arms on their tummy. Slowly sway from side to side.

2. Change position: hold the child over one shoulder and gently tip yourself forward and up again – holding on very tight!

3. Pick up the child under both arms and ensure they face outwards. Swing them gently between your legs as high as is comfortable and safe for you both.

4. Keep holding the child under their arms and spin in a circle. Not too fast!

What's in it for the children?

All these movements support the development of the vestibular system (located in the inner ear and linked to balance and coordination). This links to skills children will need later on, e.g. the ability to sit still. It is vitally important that their early experience of being physically active with adults is positive and enjoyable.

Taking it forward

- As children become increasingly mobile and more physically confident and competent, encourage them to swing, sway and twirl independently. They could twirl to music and use light props, e.g. chiffon scarves or a ribbon.

50 fantastic ideas for getting children active

Sand play (small scale)

Dig, pour, scoop or drizzle

What you need:

- A sheet
- A washing up bowl, filled halfway with sand
- Selection of small hand apparatus

What to do:

1. Invite the child to join you comfortably around the bowl. They may choose to sit, stand, kneel or squat.

2. Encourage the child to decide independently which materials to work with. Initially just have a selection of small familiar materials, e.g. teaspoons, tea strainers, egg cups, wooden spoons, scoops, containers or jugs.

3. Suggest inviting another child to participate to encourage sharing of resources and positive interactions.

4. Encourage children to use a range of manipulative skills to dig, pour, scoop, pat or drizzle the sand. Reinforce the appropriate vocabulary linked to each hand skill.

5. Try to maintain a muted presence and encourage children to follow their own ideas.

6. Encourage children to change position frequently around the bowl: from sitting, to standing, to kneeling, to squatting.

7. Children may wish to push or pull the bowl to another place. Allow them to do so unaided.

What's in it for the children?

Changing position frequently around the bowl, or pushing or pulling the bowl along the floor, supports children's balance, agility and overall body strength. Independent decision-making is encouraged as children engage with the resources alone or with others.

Taking it forward

- Hide small objects in the sand. The children can try to find them with their fingers at first, then by using teaspoons.

- Add water to the sand and explore all the new possibilities offered for shape-making and construction.

Cruise control

Sit and bounce with chairs

What you need:

- A basic kitchen chair or stool

What to do:

1. Allow the children to explore all the properties of the chair, e.g. size, shape and texture.

2. Encourage the children to crawl underneath the chair and sit very still underneath it for a few seconds.

3. Ask the children to put both of their hands on the seat of the chair and pat it very loudly, then very softly. You could cover a child's hands with yours to fix them in place initially, then take your hands away very quickly.

4. Explore making sounds using different hand movements on the chair, e.g. bang, rub, pound, knock or scratch. Repeat the sounds you and the children like best.

5. Encourage the children to stand and bounce up and down, holding on to the chair for support.

6. Encourage them to clamber onto the chair unaided or with help and sit still for a few moments.

7. Carefully help the children to jump down, supporting them under their armpits.

What's in it for the children?

This is a good time to thoroughly explore a familiar resource and practise a range of essential body movements, e.g. stretching and bouncing. Engaging with a chair supports children's proprioceptive sense and presents opportunities to explore making different sounds and rhythms.

Taking it forward

- Find different objects and invite the children to put them under, on or beside the chair. This is an opportunity to rehearse prepositional language in a relevant and meaningful context.

Suitcase beds
Curl up in a suitcase!

What you need:

- A selection of different sized suitcases lined with soft fabric.

What to do:

1. Encourage the children to explore the properties of the suitcase beds as they crawl into and lie down in them on their backs and tummies. Allow time for exploration and experimentation. Try not to interfere: just observe and join in if and when appropriate.

2. Let the children push and pull the suitcase beds around the space.

3. Invite the children to help move the suitcase beds from one place to another. Let the children explore different pockets, open and close the lids and zip them up.

4. Encourage the children to find objects they can put in the suitcase beds, such as soft toys.

50 fantastic ideas for getting children active

What's in it for the children?

A wide range of big body movements may be practised here, such as pushing and pulling, crawling and stretching. The proprioceptive sense is stimulated as children discover if they can fit into the spaces of the different sized suitcase beds.

Taking it forward

- Use the beds as moveable calm spaces that children can sit or lie inside. You could read a story or sing together during this time.

Sponges in water

What happens to a sponge in water?

What you need:

- A small container of water (not too full) e.g. a washing-up bowl
- A selection of small sponges of different shapes, colours and sizes
- A plastic sheet to place the container on

What to do:

1. Invite the children to choose a dry sponge. Talk about the shapes and colours available.

2. Ask the children to place their sponge lightly on the surface of the water and watch it float. They could gently push it around the bowl or try blowing it to see if it will move just as well.

3. Now ask the children to place one hand flat on the sponge and push it under the water, then take their hand away and watch it rise to the surface.

4. Repeat this action until the sponge is saturated and begins to sink.

5. Ask the children to lift their sponge out of the water with both hands and drop it back in so it makes a splash, then repeat.

6. Help the children to take off their shoes and socks and carefully climb into the bowl and step on the sponges while keeping as upright as possible.

What's in it for the children?

Children use both their hands and feet to engage with a familiar resource and practise a range of physical skills. This activity can be used to introduce the concepts of same/different, wet/dry and light/heavy.

Taking it forward

- Consider introducing a wider range of hand movements, e.g. wringing or twisting, using each hand independently.

- Using the damp sponges as art materials, encourage the children to make large patterns on a chalk board.

Scramble up and stand

Stand up and flop down

What you need:

- A safe, hazard-free space

Top tip ⭐

Be consistently encouraging and positive and notice how this emerging strength may affect children's level of competence and confidence when engaging in other activities.

What's in it for the children?

This is so useful for supporting overall body strength, agility and balance. Children use all the big muscle groups together as they pull themselves up and bounce on their feet. This is very effective preparation for future fluent walking.

Taking it forward

- Bounce together to some music or your favourite song.

- Be aware when children are ready to start 'cruising' round the furniture and clambering over it. This is a really important stage and must be properly supported: ensure they cannot pull anything over, e.g. a tablecloth.

What to do:

1. Encourage the children to scramble up to standing by themselves from lying on their backs or tummies. Encourage them to either hold on to you (or the sides of a cot) as they pull themselves up.

2. Encourage energetic bouncing on their feet as they stand.

3. Let the children flop onto their bottoms and pull themselves up again.

4. Allow lots of time to repeat this movement without help.

Pillow play (upper body)

Upper body movements with pillows

What you need:

- A pillow or cushion with a pillow-case or cover on it, one per child
- A large container such as a wash basket

What to do:

1. Invite the children to take their pillows to a space they have chosen.
2. Ask them to use both hands to pat the pillows as hard as possible.
3. Ask them to make their hands into fists and pummel the pillows very fast.
4. Invite the children to poke and prod the pillows all over, using their 'pointy' fingers.
5. Invite them to lie on the pillows and squash them flat, then get up and puff them up again. Repeat this activity a few times and encourage the children to try lying on both their tummies and backs.
6. Ask the children to try to stuff all the pillows into the container.

Top tip

Children always have great ideas for engaging with pillows, so try to go along with them whenever possible.

What's in it for the children?

All these activities promote strength and upper body coordination.

Taking it forward

- Source a range of soft toys and see how many they can fit between the pillow and the pillowcase.
- Use the pillow as a bed for the toys and tuck a few under the pillowcase to sleep.

Pillow play (lower body)

Lower body movements with pillows

What you need:

- A pillow or cushion with a pillowcase or cover on it, one per child

What's in it for the children?

Activities with pillows are a very effective way to support all-over body strength, balance and coordination in a safe and manageable way.

Taking it forward

- Line up the pillows: can the children crawl or walk over them unaided?
- Invite the children to stack the pillows before trying, in turn, to climb onto the pile unaided.

What to do:

1. Ask the children to take their shoes off and stand on the pillows unaided with their feet together and arms stretched above their heads.

2. Encourage them to stamp their feet as hard as possible on the pillows.

3. Ask the children to try and jump on the pillows with their feet together, then to try jumping onto the pillows landing on their knees.

4. Invite the children to sit on the floor and push the pillows around with their feet.

5. Now ask them to flop onto the pillows landing on their tummies to squash them flat.

6. Ask the children to pick up the pillows and throw them in the air as high or as far as possible.

Beanbags underfoot

Crawling over uneven surfaces

What you need:

- A single bed sheet or blanket
- A selection of small beanbags or small soft toys

What's in it for the children?

By using hands and feet to find hidden objects, children's spatial awareness and spatial memory are challenged. Their balance and coordination are also supported as they crawl and walk unaided over the beanbags.

Taking it forward

- Make the beanbags more challenging to find, e.g. place them around the perimeter of the sheet.
- Spread the beanbags out more widely so stepping from one to the other is more difficult.
- Ask the children to find particular beanbags or soft toys under the sheet – in a specific order – or tell them to find two of the same colour.
- Use a patterned sheet to make finding the beanbags more difficult.

What to do:

1. Scatter a selection of small beanbags evenly on the floor. Encourage the children to choose where and how to place them.
2. Encourage the children to handle the beanbags with both hands and use different hand movements as they carefully pat the bags.
3. Talk to the children about the colours they have chosen: do they have a favourite colour?
4. With the children's help unfold the sheet and place it over all the beanbags.
5. Invite the children to take their shoes off and crawl over the sheet to find and pat the beanbags underneath.
6. Encourage the children to step from one beanbag to another unaided and squash the bags with their feet.

Dressing teddies

Choosing clothes for a teddy

What you need:

- A teddy for each child
- A selection of teddy/doll clothes, hats and scarves

What's in it for the children?

Children practise decision-making and collaboration. They use a wide range of manipulative skills. There are lots of opportunities to relate this activity to personal circumstances, e.g. 'Does everyone need to wear…?' or 'My mum/dad/nan has…'

Taking it forward

- Make the materials more challenging, e.g. smaller buttons, hooks and eyes.

- Introduce a time restriction, e.g. say 'In five minutes from now all the teddies need to be wearing…'

- Create more physically challenging stories for children to imagine with their teddies: climbing Everest, swimming with sharks or travelling by magic carpet or hot-air balloon!

What to do:

1. Place the clothes on a sheet.

2. Hide the teddies in the space and ask the children to find them and bring them to the sheet. Each child should choose a teddy to dress.

3. Encourage discussion about what may fit or suit each teddy.

4. Encourage the children to move around as they choose materials for their teddies.

5. When the teddies are dressed, discuss the experience. Are any teddies dressed for wet weather or sunshine? If the teddies are going on holiday, what would they need to pack?

6. Introduce a story that encourages the children to be physically active with their teddies, such as going on a bear hunt, going on holiday, or preparing for a storm. As you tell the story, the children can move with their bears, for example stretching, jumping, lying down or pretending to hide.

 Health & Safety
Ensure there are no stray fastenings that could be swallowed.

Blanket time

Experiment with movement on blankets

What you need:

- A light blanket

What to do:

1. Invite the children to help you spread the blanket out neatly on the floor.

2. Ask them to lie very still on their backs on one half of the blanket with their arms and legs together and stretched out as long as possible.

3. Slowly cover up the children's feet with the rest of the blanket, followed by their legs, tummies and chests, describing what you are doing.

4. Play peek-a-boo when you get to their heads.

5. Spread the blanket out again and ask the children to remain very still as you pull them around the room on the blanket (no more than two or three children at a time).

6. Now invite them to sit up or kneel on the blanket. Can they balance upright as you pull them around? Wiggle the blanket from side to side to further challenge their overall strength and balancing ability.

7. Roll up the blanket into a sausage shape and ask the children to sit or lie on it.

8. Put the ends of the sausage shape together to make a circle. Put some familiar toys in the middle and invite the children to be inside the circle all together for a short while.

What's in it for the children?

There are lots of opportunities presented here for supporting language and communication. Overall body strength, balance and coordination are supported throughout the activities.

Taking it forward

- Can the children help fold the blanket or stuff it into a container?

- Roll objects up inside the blanket. Can the children remember how to unfold the blanket to find them again?

In and out

Fun with bottle tops

What you need:

- A large box or container, filled with plastic bottle tops (different colours and sizes)
- Small containers, e.g. yogurt pots

What's in it for the children?

Children practise big body movements when sitting and standing in the box and use a range of essential hand movements.

Taking it forward

- Ask the children to identify different colours and sort the bottle tops into piles.
- Encourage them to create different shapes and patterns with the bottle tops on the floor, e.g. snakes, roads, flowers, trucks, or circles, lines and squares.
- Think of different sounds and rhythms you can make with the bottle tops, starting with a single top and then adding more. For example, tapping them on the floor or rubbing two tops together. Invite the children to really listen to the sounds and discuss how they made them.

What to do:

1. Encourage the children to use both hands to dig deep into the container full of bottle tops and swish, stir and scoop them.

2. Invite the children to transfer the bottle tops into another container, using their hands or a smaller container to transfer them.

3. Now that the large container is empty, invite children to sit inside it and other children to put the bottle tops and yogurt pots back in. They can vigorously wiggle their feet and legs as their legs are slowly covered up and 'disappear' under the bottle tops.

4. Pour all the bottle tops out of the large container again and invite children to stand very still inside it and others to fill it up. Children can wait for their ankles to be covered up by bottle tops. They can then shuffle their feet in the container to make a loud noise, keeping upright all the time!

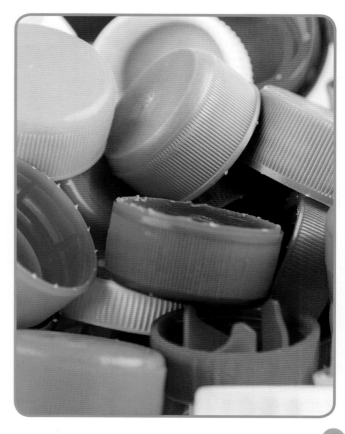

Fetch and carry

Build 'book towers'

What you need:

- Large, heavy books

What to do:

1. Present the books and encourage the children to identify a suitable place to stack them and build a tower as a group.

2. Let the children choose their own book(s) and carry them unaided to the space determined for the tower. Allow them to carry the book in any way they like, e.g. using one hand or two hands, carrying books on their heads or under their arms.

3. Encourage children to be accurate and precise as they put the books one on top of the other. Discuss why this is important: because otherwise the tower will fall down!

4. Invite the children to collaborate and communicate as the tower grows.

5. Encourage discussion about feeling strong. How many more books can they carry without getting tired? Can they carry more than one book at a time?

What's in it for the children?

Upper body strength and endurance is challenged as children carry the books from one place to another and reach up high to build the tower. This activity also encourages decision-making skills. Collaboration and communication is encouraged as children complete the task together.

Taking it forward

- Encourage the children to carry more than one book at a time: they may need to find a bag or container to do this.

- Add other resources to extend the structure, e.g. children could build the tower on a chair or table, then hide under or inside the structure.

50 fantastic ideas for getting children active

Jumper ball

Turn a jumper into a soft ball

What you need:

- A selection of old jumpers (any size)
- Masking tape

Top tip ⭐

You can make jumper balls in a variety of sizes and weights. Jumper balls are very useful because they don't roll far and are easy to throw and kick.

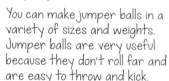

What's in it for the children?

Children collaborate and communicate as they share a single resource. The skills needed to be competent team players are practised in a supportive and manageable way.

Taking it forward

- All the classic ball skills may be introduced and practised with a jumper ball, including throwing, passing and kicking. Try not to rush into actively teaching catching or kicking. This preparatory 'ball play' time is critical to ensure later confidence and competence in a range of physical disciplines.

What to do:

1. Encourage the children to choose a jumper to make a ball. Discuss what may be a suitable size, weight, texture and pattern.

2. Invite the children to watch carefully as you fold the jumper into a ball and tape it tightly. Discuss what you are doing.

3. Invite the children to take turns carrying the ball and placing it in different positions, e.g. under a chair, on a shelf or in a box.

4. Now ask the children to sit or kneel in a circle and pass the ball from one to another. Encourage them to pass the ball in both directions around the circle, using both hands.

5. Invite children to lie on their tummies and stretch their arms forward into the middle of the circle, in order to push the ball across the middle from one to another.

6. Ask the children to sit with legs stretched forward and invite them to push the ball across the middle of the circle with their feet.

7. The adult sits in the middle of the circle and drops the ball into the lap of each child in turn, who throws or rolls it back. Progress to throwing the ball to each child in turn, encouraging them to catch with both hands.

8. Roll the ball along the floor. Each child in turn runs to pick it up and hands it back to the adult.

Tape rolls

Make shapes and structures with rolls of tape

What you need:

- A selection of masking tape rolls – wide and narrow
- A container or box

What to do:

1. Encourage the children to spend some time exploring the properties of the rolls using both hands, e.g. size, weight, shape, smell or texture.

2. Encourage the children to explore what they can do with wide and narrow rolls, e.g. they could put them on their arms like bracelets or on their heads like a crown?

3. Invite the children to make patterns on the floor, e.g. place the narrow rolls in a line, followed by the wide rolls, or they could place them in a wide circle.

4. Suggest constructing a tower using both sizes and encourage precision and accuracy as the children place one roll on top of the other.

5. Scatter the rolls on the floor and encourage the children to step carefully from one to the other while keeping their balance.

6. Source an appropriate container and encourage the children to throw the rolls with both hands or one hand into the container.

7. If you have a piece of rope or fabric available, everyone can now help thread the rolls onto the material at the end of the activity, to keep them tidy.

What's in it for the children?

This is a chance to use familiar apparatus in new and innovative ways, using a wide range of manipulative skills. Children practise decision making and collaborating in a group.

Taking it forward

- Make tasks more complex by encouraging the children to make more challenging structures or by creating patterns and sequences yourself for children to copy.

- Place a sheet over the rolls and invite children to step from one to another unaided. This requires a high degree of strength and balance.

Push and pull

Group games with one cushion

What you need:

- A large flat cushion

What to do:

1. Invite the children to sit, lie, kneel and stand on the cushion. Encourage them to change position at speed.

2. Ask the children to sit around the cushion and hide different body parts underneath it, e.g. hands or feet. How quickly can they hide these body parts? Can they think of other parts to hide?

3. Invite the children to kneel around the cushion and hold on tight to it. Now all lift it together, as high as possible, before letting it go and dropping it to the floor.

4. Try the same task, but this time ask everyone to stand as they lift and drop the cushion together. Repeat a few times until they feel tired.

5. Ask the children to carry the cushion together around the space, encouraging discussion of where to go.

6. Put the cushion on the floor and invite the children to push it along the floor all together.

7. As a group, turn the cushion upside down, over and over, at speed.

What's in it for the children?

Children use a familiar resource to practise a range of big body movements, e.g. carrying, lifting and pushing. These all support overall body strength, coordination, balance and agility. This activity encourages group work and collaboration.

Taking it forward

- Ask children to find all the teddies (or dolls) in the room and hide their heads/legs/feet in turn underneath the cushion. Then ask them to line the toys up around the edge of the cushion.

Stairs and slopes

Retrieve an object at the top

What you need:

- A beanbag or small soft toy
- A slope/short flight of stairs

What to do:

1. Identify an appropriate short flight of stairs or a slope and ask the child to choose a small beanbag or toy to use.

2. Ask the child to watch you throw the beanbag or toy a short way up the stairs/slope.

3. Say you would like them to get the object and bring it back to you.

4. Encourage the child to crawl up to retrieve it, then slide back down on their tummy.

5. Allow time for lots of repetition and for making the distance to crawl up longer and more challenging.

Top tip ★

Don't be too ambitious to begin with and encourage lots of practice. Children will probably extend the distance themselves when they are confident of success.

What's in it for the children?

Practising on manageable small slopes and slides builds the necessary confidence and competence to successfully and safely tackle larger apparatus later on.

Taking it forward

- Throw the beanbag or toy a bit higher and count the stairs as you do so.

- Invite children to throw the object by themselves.

✚ Health & Safety

Don't throw the object too far initially and ensure children slide down on their tummies.

Magazines

Make a road, zigzag or slalom with magazines

What you need:

- A selection of magazines of different sizes and weights

What to do:

1. Ask the children to pick up the magazines one by one and place them end to end on the floor to make a long straight 'road'.

2. Ask them to tiptoe carefully and quietly along the road, then stamp very hard as they walk.

3. Try stepping on every other magazine while moving forwards, taking big strides.

4. Invite the children to crawl as fast as possible around the road. At a signal, e.g. a clap, ask them to place a specific body part on a magazine, e.g. their elbows or bottoms.

5. Invite the children to change the pattern of the magazines to make a zigzag or slalom, leaving wide gaps. Invite them to weave in and out on their hands or knees.

6. Scatter the magazines and invite the children to take big steps from one to another without touching the floor.

7. Invite the children to choose a magazine to sit on for a few moments.

What's in it for the children?

Children engage with familiar apparatus in new and innovative ways.

Taking it forward

- Create more complex shapes and patterns with the magazines. Children can start to recognise particular numbers, letters, colours and shapes on the covers.

Bags of fun

Paper bags: the most versatile resource!

What you need:

- Plain paper bags (e.g. sandwich bags), one per child

What to do:

1. Ask the children to put their paper bag on the floor and place both hands flat on top of it. Invite them to tap their fingers lightly on the bag, then strongly.

2. Ask the children to scratch the bag with their fingers, keeping their wrists on the bag the whole time.

3. Now start moving! Ask the children to spread their hands wide on the bag and put their bottoms in the air before pushing the bag around the floor without bumping into each other.

4. Ask the children to stand up and place one foot on the bag, in order to begin to 'skate' around, using their right and left feet in turn, without bumping into other children.

5. Invite the children to put all the bags on the floor and step from one bag to another without touching the floor.

6. Ask the children to pick up a bag and crumple it into a small ball, before smoothing it out flat again, using both hands then one hand only.

7. Invite the children to cup the ball in both hands and throw it as high as possible, then pick it up off the floor and repeat.

8. Invite the children to put the ball between their feet and squeeze it in place. Then see if they can try jumping on the spot or jumping forwards, keeping the bag in place.

9. Encourage the children to dribble the bag around the floor, using both feet and avoiding other children.

What's in it for the children?

Children gain experience of engaging with familiar apparatus in innovative ways, using a wide range of physical skills that support overall strength, balance and coordination.

Taking it forward

- Scatter the bags on the floor and ask the children to try to blow them in different directions.

- Invite the children to kick or throw the balls underarm or overarm towards a designated target.

Cups

Shapes and patterns with cups

What you need:

- **Disposable plastic cups, one per child plus a few spares**
- **A table**

What's in it for the children?

Children explore their understanding of shape, pattern and number and have lots of opportunities for collaboration and discussion. Fine motor skills are challenged: light cups need careful handling.

Taking it forward

- Consider more challenging patterns and structures for children to make.

- Explore making different sounds with the cups, e.g. by tapping, scrunching, or flicking them.

- Create more complex table games, e.g. roll a marble across the table and ask the children to catch it with their cups.

✚ Health & Safety

Don't use paper cups: children can bite bits off and may swallow them!

What to do:

1. Invite the children to place the cups in a scatter formation on the floor, rims facing down.

2. Ask them to quickly place the cups in a straight line, with no gaps.

3. Scatter the cups again and ask the children to put them in a circle shape as quickly as possible. Repeat this activity with different shapes.

4. Ask them to stack the cups.

5. Ask the children to scatter the cups around, base down, before stacking the cups again.

6. Create a simple pattern with the cups on the floor (some cups rim down and some base down). Invite the children to make the same pattern themselves.

7. Ask the children to make a structure together with the cups, any way they like. Encourage discussion about the shape and height of the structure and encourage precision and accuracy as they place the cups.

8. Put a few cups rim down on a clear table and invite the children to blow the cups off, then replace and repeat the activity.

Got rhythm?

Make a road, zigzag or slalom with magazines

What you need:

- A selection of materials that may be used to create rhythms

Top tip ⭐

It's good for children to see you enjoying making rhythms and moving to music! They won't be critical and laughing together is so important.

What's in it for the children?

Creating rhythms supports a range of manipulative skills and the timing ability necessary for later engagement in many sports.

Taking it forward

- Create more complex rhythmical patterns with the resources.

- Discuss with the children what their favourite rhymes and songs are. Say or sing them together and use small implements to reinforce the rhythmic element.

What to do:

1. Encourage the children to make rhythms with their hands, by clapping or tapping, knocking and banging on different surfaces.

2. Introduce small, familiar implements, e.g. a teaspoon, pencil or toothbrush.

3. Introduce larger materials, such as an upturned washing up bowl, saucepan or mug. Children could pat these with their hands or bang them with an implement to create different rhythms.

4. Try to use your voice rhythmically and create rhymes that children may absorb and repeat independently.

Wheels

Try out moving on wheels

What you need:

- A selection of wheeled resources: balance bikes, scooters, tummy boards, skateboards, pedal bikes, or wheelbarrows

What to do:

1. Give the children plenty of time to explore all the movement possibilities offered by a range of wheeled resources.

2. Encourage the children to try as many different resources as possible – not just their favourites – as each resource requires different physical skills to manage and challenges varied muscle groups.

3. Encourage any interesting new ideas for using the apparatus: the obvious ones may not be the most creative or collaborative.

50 fantastic ideas for getting children active

What's in it for the children?

Children get ample time and space to explore the different resources – alone or with friends. They use all the large muscle groups to move in different directions and at varying speeds. Using both hands and feet to pedal, push and pull backwards and forwards supports overall body strength and coordination.

Taking it forward

- Encourage children to create obstacle courses to move around by pedalling, pulling or pushing.

- Introduce a time element. How long does it take to complete the obstacle course, by pedalling, pulling or pushing?

 **Health & Safety**

Ensure all the resources are appropriate for the children's level of confidence and competence.

Sock ideas

Making patterns with socks

What you need:

- Around 20 socks stored in a bag (different sizes, textures, colours and types)

What's in it for the children?

Engaging with a familiar resource presents a wealth of opportunities to explore space, shape and pattern in an active way. Positive verbal interaction is encouraged as the children discuss the properties of the socks.

Taking it forward

- Make more complex patterns and shapes with the socks (flat and rolled up).

- Practise batting, throwing or kicking the sock balls. Create a target or goal to aim at.

What to do:

1. Invite the children to join you in taking the socks one by one out of the bag. Discuss who they may belong to (a child or adult?) and the different sizes, colours and textures.

2. Ask the children to place all the socks in a line along the floor, encouraging discussion as to which socks should be placed together, e.g. arranged by colour or pattern.

3. Invite the children to lie down one by one alongside the line. How many children are needed to match the length of the line?

4. Now ask the children to choose another shape to make with the socks, e.g. a star or zigzag shape. Ensure everyone has their say.

5. Ask the children to make the widest circle they can using all the socks. Can everyone fit inside the shape if they lie, kneel, sit or stand in it?

6. All the children sit/kneel/squat around the edge of the circle and place both hands on a sock. Choose one child at a time to run around the circle and back to their sock. Repeat this going in the other direction and allow the children to take as many turns as they like.

7. Make socks into balls – one for each child – and ask the children to crawl around the floor as they pat them.

8. Find a small container and ask the children to put the sock balls into it as fast as possible. Have some spare sock balls handy to make this more challenging and repeat a few times until the children are a bit puffed!

Local parkour

Find your own obstacle course

What you need:

- A park or playground

What's in it for the children?

Children engage closely with the outdoor environment in a physically challenging way. Many opportunities are offered that support overall body strength, balance, coordination and agility. Concepts of direction, space and speed are experienced in a relevant and meaningful way.

Taking it forward

- Identify and explore any further possibilities offered by the environment that could encourage big body movements.

What to do:

1. Identify appropriate resources in the immediate outdoor environment that the children can safely engage with, e.g. a low wall, tyres, benches, trees or a gentle slope. Look for obstacles that can be balanced on, run around, walked along or climbed on.

2. Focus on one resource at a time and invite the children to engage closely with it. For example, start by sitting on a bench, then lie along it, crawl underneath it or climb onto and jump off it.

3. Introduce a sequencing element by adding another resource, e.g. jump off the bench, then run around a tree.

4. Add another two or three resources to the sequence, so ultimately the children have created their own parkour course. For example, jump off the bench, then run around the tree, then walk along the low wall, then jump into the tyre.

5. Encourage the children to decide how to complete the course and what speed is best for them.

Obstacle courses
Obstacles inside or outside

What you need:

- Familiar materials e.g. a table, chairs, cushions, blankets, a large bag or box, swimming rings

Top tip ⭐

It may take time for some children to build up to the level of competence and confidence needed to complete a whole course independently. Some children may need to just watch or simply touch the resources for a period before participating fully. Some may also feel more comfortable initially engaging with only one or two familiar pieces.

✚ Health & Safety

Always leave a suitable gap between each child as they move along the course. If indoors, it's best to take shoes off. Never put anything soft before something hard, e.g. a cushion before a table (if they fall over the cushion they may hit the table hard).

What to do:

1. Ask the children to decide what resources they want to use to construct their course, inside or outdoors. Encourage discussion as the children select their resources and put them in a linear formation. It's good to have a mix of materials that require different actions, e.g. pulling, climbing, jumping, crawling or balancing, and to make a course that may be started from either end.

2. Allow the children to approach and complete their course unaided if possible.

3. Be clear what they should do when they reach the end: restart immediately or wait for everyone to finish?

4. Let the children have as many turns as they like – some children will tire sooner than others.

What's in it for the children?

Obstacle courses provide a positive experience of individual decision-making. All the large muscle groups are used, promoting overall body strength, agility, coordination and balance.

Taking it forward

- Include different balance positions, e.g. standing on a chair with feet together and arms stretched high, or sitting on a table holding knees tight to chest.

- Ask the children what they enjoyed, what they found challenging, and what further equipment they could use next time.

- This is excellent preparation for local parkour (page 39).

Mystery objects

Hide and seek with mystery objects

What you need:

- Small familiar objects (e.g. pencil, spoon, bead and button) wrapped in tin foil or another material to hide them
- A box or bag

What to do:

1. Hide the objects in reasonably accessible places in the immediate environment.
2. Encourage the children to search for them and give everyone a chance to find a few. Encourage discussion and collaboration within the group and invite children to use a wide range of movements during their search, e.g. stretching, crawling, climbing and carrying.
3. When they find an object, ask children to place it in the box or bag.
4. When all objects are collected, invite the children to sit together to discuss what they think the objects could be.
5. Unwrap each object and see if they guessed correctly.

What's in it for the children?

This activity encourages closer engagement with the immediate environment. Social skills are stimulated and supported as children wait their turn and help each other. There are lots of possibilities for language development, as children discuss what the mystery objects could be.

Taking it forward

- Use more unfamiliar objects, e.g. a wristwatch or sink plug.
- Make the hiding places more challenging, e.g. between books on the shelf.
- Include a time element, e.g. find three items in 30 seconds.

Sticky tape challenge

'Catch' sticky tape strips on a wall

What you need:

- **A wide roll of masking tape**
- **A clear wall**

What to do:

1. Stick three strips of masking tape in horizontal lines on a clear wall. The first strip should be placed at the average tummy height of the children, the second at average top-of-head height and the final should be placed about 30 centimetres higher than the rest.

2. Invite the children to lie on their backs with both feet touching the foot of the wall. They then walk their feet up the wall to touch the lowest strip. Repeat this with the middle strip and see how close they can get to the top one. They will need to wiggle and change position! Repeat the activity until they feel tired.

3. Ask the children to lie with their toes touching the wall, but this time they bend their knees and put their arms above their heads. Ask them to sit up and touch the bottom and middle strips with their hands. How often can they do this sit-up action before getting tired?

4. Ask the children to stand and try to touch the top strip of tape. Encourage them to really stretch and jump if necessary.

Top tip ⭐

You may need to organise children into groups of a similar height to ensure everyone can join in equally.

What's in it for the children?

This is an effective way of introducing physical challenges in a small space.

Taking it forward

- Invite children to put their hands on the floor, facing away from the wall with their tummies pointing down. Ask them to try to walk their feet backwards up the wall, starting slowly by lifting one foot, then the other, eventually taking their entire body weight on their hands.

- When children are on their feet, create a competition. How many times can they jump and touch the top strip of tape in a given time?

Angels in the 'snow'

Making angels on the floor

What you need:

- Space for children to lie down and spread out without touching others

What's in it for the children?

This is an easy way to encourage big body movements in a safe and manageable way. Using the whole body in one complete movement synchronises upper and lower body actions. Overall strength and coordination is supported and children's timing ability is challenged too.

Taking it forward

- Combine making 'angels' with other movements, e.g. finish with a big jump then lie down again.

- Introduce a time restriction, e.g. 'How many angel movements can you do in 30 seconds?'

- Split the children into groups. Each group has a turn to see how many angels and jumps they can do within a given time limit.

What to do:

1. Carefully describe the 'snow angel' movement you are looking for and demonstrate if appropriate.

2. Tell the children that this movement is often called 'angels in the snow'. They should lie on their backs and move their arms and legs together out and in, in one big synchronised movement.

3. Repeat this movement up to ten times, at different speeds. For example, very fast or very slow.

4. Ask the children to try doing this movement on their tummies.

Duvet tunnels

Sliding or crawling under duvets

What you need:

- **A double lightweight duvet**

What's in it for the children?

Children need to use their overall body strength, agility and coordination to move on their tummies. Confidence and competence will be gained through practice and repetition. Using duvets is a good way to build up to bigger and more challenging tunnels that children may encounter in outdoor or adventure playgrounds.

Taking it forward

- Unfold the duvet to make a longer 'tunnel' to crawl under.

- Source different materials to crawl under, e.g. a blanket, sheet of lycra or a parachute.

What to do:

1. Encourage the children to help you fold the duvet in half widthways.

2. Ask the children to help you place it on the floor in a space that is safe and clean.

3. Now ask the children to get onto their tummies and 'commando crawl' using their elbows and toes to help propel them underneath the duvet from one end to the other.

4. Encourage the children to try 'salamander slithering'. This means moving backwards on their tummies using their arms and hands to push their bodies along.

Top tip

Children may need to start gently, putting just their heads under the duvet at first, then gradually building up the confidence to put their whole body under.

Health & Safety

Ensure the duvet is as lightweight as possible and that there are no fraying edges or holes in it.

Table time

Use a table for a stop/start game

What you need:

- One table (or two tables placed end to end)
- Space to run around the tables

What to do:

1. Ask the children to all place their right hands on the table and stand facing forwards. Ensure they are evenly spaced around the table and have adequate room to move around it.

2. Explain carefully that they are to run around the table keeping one hand touching it at all times. Aim for the children to move for maximum 15 seconds at a time before you use a 'stop' signal, e.g. clap or say 'freeze!'

3. Now ask the children to put their left hand on the table and move in the other direction. Repeat until they feel a bit puffed.

4. Ask the children to make a 'tower' of hands together by putting their hands one on top of the other in the middle of the table.

5. Ask the children to place both hands flat on the table for support as they jump on the spot, first with their feet together, then apart.

6. Change the action to hopping: one foot, then the other.

7. Still using the table for support, ask the children to lift one leg as high as possible behind them and hold this balance before swapping legs.

8. Invite the children to lie across the table, lift their arms and legs and balance for a moment. Ensure there is space for everyone!

Top tip ★

Ensure children know precisely what the 'stop' or 'freeze' signal is before they start moving.

What's in it for the children?

Table activities are useful preparation for team sports. Children develop their body strength, coordination, agility and balance as they practise big body movements. Their proprioceptive sense is also supported as they have to be very aware of the space they're moving in.

Taking it forward

- Encourage faster changes of direction.

- Ask children to try different 'swimming strokes' while lying on the table, e.g. doggy paddle or breaststroke.

Socks on hands

Stretch and squeeze hands inside socks

What you need:

- A selection of clean socks (different colours, sizes, textures, types)

What's in it for the children?

Using socks encourages hand strength and manipulative skills that are linked to later fluent hand-writing. Closer engagement with their immediate environment is encouraged as they engage with different surfaces.

Taking it forward

- Make different shapes or patterns with the socks on the floor, e.g. line them up end to end to make a 'road', a circle, a star or a snake shape.
- Make interesting 'feely-bags' by putting a variety of easily recognisable or more challenging objects inside the socks for children to discover.

What to do:

1. Tip the socks into a pile on the floor and ask the children to find a pair they like. Encourage the children to discuss the reasons for their choice.

2. Help the children to put a sock on each hand.

3. Ask them to stretch, wiggle and squeeze their hands inside the socks. A wide range of movements are possible with socks on hands: be creative! Encourage the children to make 'sad', 'happy' or 'cross' faces, e.g. by scrunching their hands into a fist for 'cross'.

4. Demonstrate, then encourage the children to rub, 'clean' or 'polish' different parts of their bodies, e.g. their heels, elbows or armpits. Then extend the idea to the immediate environment, e.g. the floor, wall or windowsill. Find some tricky corners! Encourage the children to really stretch and rub vigorously using both hands.

5. Ask the children to place both hands on the floor (taking their bodyweight on their hands) and push themselves around the floor either on hands and knees or hands and feet.

Balloon piñata

A small group activity with balloons

What you need:

- Around seven colourful balloons, inflated half full
- String
- Small implements to 'bat' the balloons with

Top tip ⭐

Some children may be wary of balloons, so introduce this activity carefully. Start by hanging one balloon from an easily accessible height.

What's in it for the children?

This activity encourages hand-to-eye coordination, sequencing and timing ability. Overall strength is supported as children stretch, jump and bat.

Taking it forward

- Stipulate which colour balloons the children should bat, or give children an order or pattern in which to bat the balloons, e.g. white, blue, red, green.
- Organise a game with two groups of four children. Each child in the group must follow the colour sequence as fast as possible.

➕ **Health & Safety**

Only blow the balloons half full. No more than four children should participate in this activity at a time.

What to do:

1. Allow the children to watch you prepare this activity by blowing up the balloons (only half full) and then string them up on a piece of string that you hang across the middle of a room. Place the balloons at regular intervals along the string and hang the string at a height that the children can reach.

2. When the balloons are correctly positioned, encourage the children to pat each one with both hands. Ensure balloons are not patted too hard – demonstrate if appropriate.

3. Lift the string a bit higher and give each child a small implement to bat the balloons with, e.g. a wooden spoon, toothbrush, or ruler. They may have to jump to reach them.

DVD cases
Shapes and structures

What you need:

- 10 – 20 empty DVD cases with age-appropriate covers
- Optional: Toy cars, trains or marbles

What to do:

1. Tip the cases onto the floor and encourage the children to place them in a line along the base of a wall.
2. Suggest stacking the cases vertically up the wall. How high can they go and how precise must they be?
3. Suggest placing them in a pattern along the base of the wall.
4. Encourage the children to place all the cases in a scatter formation on the floor and suggest they make different shapes, e.g. a square, rectangle, or triangle.
5. Encourage the children to sort the boxes into different groups, e.g. by colour, or what's on the cover. Encourage discussion about their decisions.
6. Now open up all the cases (making a tent shape) and invite the children to place them on the floor end to end to make a tunnel. You could source some small cars or marbles that could be rolled through the tunnel.
7. Ask them to put their hands on the cases and push themselves forward around the floor, being careful not to bump into anyone.

What's in it for the children?

These cases are lighter and easier to handle than wooden bricks and therefore present a wider range of movement opportunities. Many provocations for language and communication are inherent in this resource.

Taking it forward

- Make constructions more complex, e.g. can children make a staircase using the cases to make steps of different heights?

Tights

A small group activity with a giant elastic band

What you need:

- Nylon tights in different colours and patterns, tied together to make a large elastic band, one pair per child

What to do:

1. Ask the children to stand in a circle, all holding on to the band of tights with both hands in an overhand grip.

2. Invite the children to shuffle backwards, stretching the band as wide as possible before everyone lets go to watch it 'ping' into the middle. Repeat.

3. Place the band on the floor in a large circle. Invite the children to walk, run, skip, hop, jump or gallop around the outside of the band. On a given signal, such as a clap, everyone jumps into the middle and sits down.

4. Ask the children to sit in a circle, holding onto the band, and 'feeding' it through both hands. Start slowly, then speed up.

5. Still sitting down, ask the children to stretch the band over their feet or their knees, or under their armpits. Can the group stand up and sit down all together while keeping the shape?

6. Ask the children to move around as a group while keep holding of the band in any way they choose. Encourage discussion about direction and speed.

What's in it for the children?

This activity encourages cooperation, collaboration and spatial awareness, while using an easily-accessible resource.

Taking it forward

- Use the band to explore questions of space, e.g. by asking 'How many of us can fit into this circle?' or shape, e.g. by saying 'Let's make a square/oval'.

- Unravel the band and use the tights individually, allowing the children to explore, stretching, pulling and making 'tails'.

Tambourine time

Make a paper tambourine

What you need:

- At least two paper plates (the same size)
- Masking tape
- A selection of 'fillings', e.g. beans, lentils, or paper clips

What to do:

1. Stick two paper plates together with masking tape, leaving a gap so you can pour in the filling.

2. Ask the children to choose a suitable filling from a couple of options.

3. Pour a small cup of the chosen filling into the opening and tape the plates securely shut. You now have a tambourine!

4. Invite the children to shake, tap, or bang the tambourine using both hands. How many sounds can they make using a variety of hand movements? Encourage the children to use the immediate environment (e.g. the floor or wall) and their bodies (e.g. knees or toes).

5. Source some appropriate music for jumping. Invite the children to practise all the jumps they know, e.g. feet together/apart or backwards/forwards/side to side as they bang their tambourines high and low in time to the beat.

What's in it for the children?

Children explore sounds and rhythms with big body movements. Communication and decision-making skills are practised as you and the children make the instruments together.

Taking it forward

- Make more tambourines over time, so you have a wide range of sounds to work with. You could change the 'fillings' or mix them up.

- Encourage children to explore different rhythms together with the tambourines and make them more complex and challenging, e.g. by linking to a song they already know.

- Develop a short movement routine that may be accompanied by the tambourines.

Bottle shakers

Getting active with music bottles

What you need:

- Empty plastic bottles, ideally different shapes, colours and sizes
- Materials with which to fill the bottles, e.g. beans or paper clips

What to do:

1. Ask the children to sort the bottles into groups, e.g. by size, or what's on the label. Encourage discussion.

2. Ask the children to explore what different sounds they can make using a range of hand movements, e.g. press, roll, tap with nails, bang on the floor, or flick with fingers.

3. Invite the children to make percussion instruments by pouring materials into the bottles.

4. Choose different big body movements to move to with the bottle, e.g. hold both ends and stretch up as high as possible, then touch the floor. Repeat at speed.

5. Hold onto both ends and tip the bottle one way and the other. Encourage the children to lean over as far as they can both ways. Try doing this very fast.

6. Jump with the bottle holding it tight to the chest.

7. What different weather sounds can the children make with their bottles? E.g. shake vigorously to create a 'storm'.

What's in it for the children?

Bottles offer a wide range of opportunities to explore rhythm, sound and space, in an active and collaborative way. Fine motor skills are challenged as they choose materials to put in their bottles.

Taking it forward

- Sing 'Ten green bottles' together as you take one bottle away at a time.
- Play a game with two groups. Line up the bottles against a wall. Invite the first group to run, one by one, and place the bottles flat on the floor. Invite the second group to run, one by one, to stand all the bottles up again.

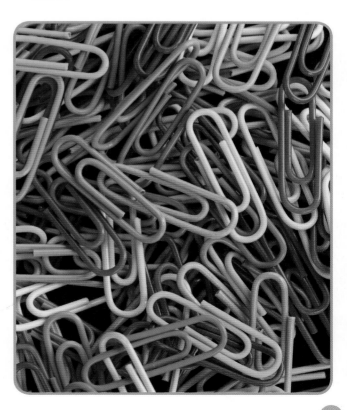

Rope snake

Stop the rope snake from moving!

What you need:

- Nylon rope (ideally 3–4 centimetres thick and 3–5 metres long)

Top tip ⭐

Start with simple activities until children are completely comfortable with the rope. It's helpful if the children are of similar height and size so they can engage equally.

What's in it for the children?

These activities require a high level of cooperation and collaboration, spatial awareness, timing ability and coordination. Upper and lower body strength, agility and balance are also challenged.

Taking it forward

- With adult support, hold the rope high in the air and ask the children to stretch or jump to catch it.

- With adult support, hold the rope above the children's heads. Place a sock over the rope at one end and ask the children to hold the ends of the sock tightly together and run from one end of the rope to the other, holding onto the sock.

What to do:

1. Invite the children to help you place the rope on the floor in a straight line.

2. Ask the children to pick up the rope together and walk forwards around the space. Change the 'leader' so everyone gets a go.

3. Place the rope back on the floor and invite the children to make different shapes with it, e.g. a circle, oval, triangle, or square. Encourage precision and discussion.

4. Place the rope in a straight line again and ask the children to walk along it facing forwards then sideways, balancing carefully.

5. Secure one end of the rope (tie to a table leg or ask another adult to hold on). Now wiggle the free end of the rope vigorously on the floor. Ask the children to stop it moving by touching it with different body parts, e.g. their feet or bottoms.

6. Invite the children to jump over the rope as it wiggles. Then ask them to jump onto it to stop it moving.

Tin cans

Shapes and games with drinks cans

What you need:

- A selection of empty drinks cans (with the openings securely taped up)

What to do:

1. Ask the children to sort the cans into different groups, e.g. according to colour, brand or what's on the label. Allow them enough time to make their own decisions.

2. Suggest they line up the cans along the base of a wall and place another layer carefully on top.

3. Ask the children to make a pyramid shape against the wall: how high can it go?

4. Invite the children to make a wide circle with the cans on the floor. Try this with the cans upright and on their sides: which makes the wider shape?

5. Ask the children to jump in and out of the circle without touching the cans: from two feet to two feet or from one foot to another foot.

6. Organise a group task. Line up the cans and ask the children to crawl as fast as possible to pick them up, before walking back to their place.

What's in it for the children?

Cans are an excellent resource for building structures. Children use very precise hand movements as they balance the cans. This is challenging with such a light resource.

Taking it forward

- Introduce more complex patterns and structures, e.g. cover a chair seat or table top with upright cans.

- Introduce a team and a time element: how quickly can the children pick up all the cans and place them in a designated container?

 Health & Safety

Ensure the cans are taped closed.

Bed sheet parachute

Keep the toy on the sheet!

What you need:

- A large double sheet
- A small soft toy

What to do:

1. Ask the children to hold onto the edge of the sheet with an overhand grip. Ensure they are evenly spaced around the sheet.

2. Ask the children to lift the sheet up and down together slowly, then as fast as possible.

3. Ask them to lift the sheet very high and then let it fall to the ground. Repeat.

4. While the children are holding the sheet high, call out each child's name in turn and ask them to run under it, to find another place.

5. Place the soft toy in the middle of the sheet. The children bounce the toy by lifting and lowering the sheet.

6. Now place the sheet flat on the floor and ask the children to kneel around the edge, placing their hands flat on the sheet. The children slide forward on their tummies until all hands meet in the middle. Then pull the sheet out flat again and repeat.

7. Ask the children to sit together and place the sheet over them. Call out each child by name and ask them to scramble out. Discuss who is still left underneath each time.

What's in it for the children?

A sheet is easier to manage than a parachute because it is smaller, lighter and more familiar. These activities allow children to build confidence and competence before engaging with larger apparatus.

Taking it forward

- The children could roll the sheet into a tube shape, then carry it or sit on it.

- Fold the sheet into different shapes: this could be an introduction to the concept of fractions.

And....breathe

Blow using paper straws

What you need:

- A table (round if possible)
- Paper straws (cut to a smaller length if necessary)
- Cotton wool balls
- A small container

What to do:

1. Ask the children to stand around the table and help you place the cotton wool balls on the table in any pattern they like, e.g. a line, scattered, or in a circle.

2. Give every child a paper straw. Invite the children to blow the balls gently around the table, making sure they don't fall off the edge.

3. Ask the children to blow as hard as possible so all the balls roll off the table. Replace the balls on the table and repeat.

4. Ask the children to use the straws to suck up the balls and place them in a small container. Scatter the balls on the table again and repeat.

What's in it for the children?

These activities are an easy, fun way to practise oral motor skills and develop breath control. There are opportunities for children to collaborate and develop their spatial awareness and sensitivity.

Taking it forward

- Add a time element: how fast can all the balls be blown off the table or transferred into the container?

- Introduce a 'goal' so there is a specific place to aim the balls at when blowing through straws.

 Health & Safety

This activity is best avoided if children have breathing difficulties. Ensure the children do not share straws.

Beach ball
Keep the ball moving!

What you need:

- A medium-sized beach ball

What to do:

1. Invite the children to watch closely as you blow up the ball and notice how it requires very deep breaths. How many breaths do they think may be needed?

2. Ask the children to lie on their tummies in a circle with their arms stretched into the middle. Ask them to push the ball across the middle with their hands, saying the name of the child they are passing to.

3. Ask the children to sit on their knees and bat the ball more forcefully across the middle of the circle, using one hand then the other.

4. Ask the children to change from their tummies to their knees at speed, while keeping the ball moving.

5. Invite the children to walk on their knees or crawl around the floor, keeping the ball moving between them by batting it with their hands. Make sure everyone gets equal turns.

6. Tell the children to walk on tiptoes around the space while carefully giving the ball to each other using both hands.

7. Now ask the children to stand in a circle and catch the ball as you throw it to each child in turn. They can jump and stretch up to catch it.

8. Invite the children to watch you deflate the ball and discuss what may be the most effective way of doing this, e.g. squeezing it or letting it deflate naturally?

50 fantastic ideas for getting children active

Top tip ⭐

Sharing one resource may be a
challenge for some children. You
could start with a small group of
three or four and slowly build up
to a bigger group.

What's in it for the children?

These activities are physically
challenging as the children change
positions at speed while keeping the
ball moving. Their spatial awareness
is developed as they move around
each other and pass the ball.

Taking it forward

- These activities are effective
  preparation for sports that involve
  passing, throwing and catching,
  particularly team sports where
  only one ball is used, e.g. netball,
  basketball or volleyball.

Umbrella houses

Play and build with umbrellas

What you need:

- Children's umbrellas, one per child
- A sheet or blanket

What to do:

1. Ask the children to imagine different weather scenarios with their umbrellas. Twirl around for a windy day, stamp in imaginary puddles or hide underneath the umbrellas during an imaginary storm, before emerging slowly to see if the rain has stopped.

2. Invite the children to use their umbrellas to make a 'house'.

3. Decide together on an appropriate place to make the house.

4. Place open umbrellas on the floor with the handles facing inwards, then overlap the umbrellas to make a cosy, secure structure. Leave a gap so the children can get inside!

5. Discuss what would be the best resources to take into the house, e.g. reading or writing materials, cooking utensils, etc.

6. Drape a sheet or light blanket over the umbrellas to secure the structure for a time.

What's in it for the children?

This is an easy way to create a personalised space – indoors or outside – that can be tidied away or moved quickly. Lots of opportunities are presented to extend language use and refine politeness rituals, as children invite others into their space.

Taking it forward

- Discuss different constructions or scenarios other than a 'house', e.g. an igloo, cave, den, tunnel or hobbit-house.

- Attach streamers to the umbrellas – they make very good jellyfish!

Health & Safety

Ensure the tips of the umbrellas are blunt. Children will need to share the space in the 'house'.

Chair gym

How many movements can you do with a chair?

What you need:

- **Chairs, one per child**

What to do:

1. Ask the children to place the chairs together in a line and sit down on them. They can then:
   a. Tap their toes on the floor, then their heels (changing between toes and heels quickly).
   b. Drum their feet on the floor.
   c. Bend their knees to lift their feet off the floor (and hold this position).
   d. Put their legs straight out in front of them, off the floor, and tap their feet together.
   e. Put their feet on the floor and bounce on their bottoms on the chair. At a given signal, e.g. a clap, the children could stand up quickly before sitting back down and bouncing again.

2. Ask the children to move up one place to the next chair. The child at the end of the line of chairs has to run to the chair at the beginning. Repeat until everyone has had a go: how fast can they complete the task?

3. With all children sitting on their chairs and holding both knees to their chests, call out one child's name. That child runs around all the chairs and back to their place. Repeat until everyone has had a go.

What's in it for the children?

Children are encouraged to be highly active in a small space using familiar equipment. Overall body strength, coordination, agility and balance is supported.

Taking it forward

- Extend the time in which children engage in continual movement, e.g. bouncing on chairs or drumming their feet.

Body shapes

Mix art with physical activity

What you need:

- A large roll of paper
- Scissors
- Pens, pencils and assorted craft materials
- Sticky tac

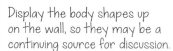

Top tip ⭐

Display the body shapes up on the wall, so they may be a continuing source for discussion.

What to do:

1. Ask the children to lie down on their backs on the paper, keeping very still with their hands by their sides.

2. Draw around each child's body, describing the body parts as you go, to reinforce vocabulary.

3. Ask each child to watch carefully as you cut around their body shape. Ask them to help you stick the shapes up on the wall.

4. Invite the children to choose their own materials to decorate their shape. Encourage discussion between the group and introduce mathematical language around size and number, e.g. 'Are your feet bigger than your hands?' or 'How much longer are your legs than your arms?'

5. Source some appropriate rhymes that you can all say and move to, e.g. 'Five little monkeys jumping on the bed', 'If you're happy and you know it' or 'Head, shoulders, knees and toes'.

What's in it for the children?

This activity is a really positive way for children to claim 'ownership' of their bodies and say 'this is me!' Many opportunities to introduce and practise new vocabulary are presented and their communication skills are challenged as they share and discuss resources.

Taking it forward

- Introduce more complex vocabulary, such as the scientific names of bones (e.g. femur) and muscles (e.g. biceps).

- Think about creating a folder for each child about their physical development, interests and abilities, e.g. 'What I am good at', 'What games/sports I like', etc. This may be added to by parents, carers, siblings and other adults they engage with. Take a picture of their decorated cut-out and use it as a cover for the folder.

Researching movement

Research and discuss physical disciplines

What you need:

- Internet access
- Optional: a printer

What to do:

1. Discuss with the children what particular movement skill (e.g. running, jumping or climbing) they would like to explore online – what interests them and why?

2. Discuss the chosen topic, for example, running:
   a. Do you like running?
   b. Are you good at running?
   c. Do your parents/carers run?
   d. Why do we run? E.g. for safety or for fun.
   e. What do you need to run effectively? E.g. balance or coordination.

3. Look online for examples of people running, e.g. Olympic athletes, marathon runners, or fell runners. You could print out pictures. What do the children notice, e.g. different speeds, clothing or terrain?

4. You could invite parents and carers to film their children running and put clips together in a short film. Invite discussion with parents and carers about how to further support children's level of physical confidence and competence.

5. Organise an active event for children and their parents and carers. Choose a few of the activities suggested in this book that parents and carers could join in with you and the children.

6. Share the children's work with parents and carers and discuss ways in which everyone can be supported to be physically active and healthy.

What's in it for the children?

Children can make connections between personal experience and a wider context. It is a good way to involve families and further encourage interest and engagement with their own and their children's physical activities.

Taking it forward

- Extend research and discussion to include dance, gymnastics, swimming or martial arts.